My Little Golder
MARTIN LUTHER
KING JR.

by Bonnie Bader
illustrated by Sue Cornelison

 A GOLDEN BOOK • NEW YORK

rhcbooks.com
Educators and librarians, for a variety of teaching tools, visit us at
RHTeachersLibrarians.com
Library of Congress Control Number: 2017948145
ISBN 978-0-525-57870-3 (trade) — ISBN 978-0-525-57871-0 (ebook)
Printed in the United States of America
10 9 8 7 6 5 4

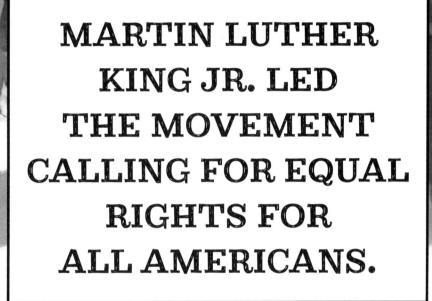

MARTIN LUTHER KING JR. LED THE MOVEMENT CALLING FOR EQUAL RIGHTS FOR ALL AMERICANS.

His boyhood home was filled with love. Martin had an older sister he called Chris and an older brother named Alfred Daniel. Their mother, Alberta, spoke softly and was kind. It was very easy for Martin to talk to her.

Martin's father, Martin Sr., was a large man with a booming voice. He was a minister of the Ebenezer Baptist Church in Atlanta, Georgia.

The church was filled with song. Martin loved music and sang in the church choir. He enjoyed Sunday school and had many friends there. Martin got along with everyone—the children, the parents, and the teachers.

But sometimes Martin's life was sad. Martin had a good friend he played with almost every day. Then, when they turned six, Martin went to a school for black children, and his friend went to a school for white children. One day, the boy's father told him he could no longer play with Martin because he was black. Heartbroken, Martin ran home and cried to his mother.

That night at dinner, Martin's parents told him it was his duty as a Christian to love everyone, even when he was angry at them.

Martin's mother also said he should always feel a sense of "somebodiness"—that he was important, even though the outside world was telling him he was not, simply because of his skin color.

In those days in the Southern United States, black people could only drink from water fountains labeled "colored." And they were not even allowed to go into many restaurants and stores.

This was called segregation—the separation of blacks from whites.

As he grew up, Martin's heart began to grow heavier and sadder. He tried to remember his mother's words, that he was somebody, that he *was* important. But it wasn't easy.

WE SERVE WHITES only

OPEN

One day, Martin's father took him shoe
shopping. Even though the store was empty,
the shopkeeper told them they had to go to
the back of the store and wait to be served.

Mr. King became angry. If he couldn't buy
shoes for his son in the front of the store, he
wouldn't buy them there at all! Taking hold
of Martin's hand, he marched out.

COLORED SERVED
IN REAR

"I don't care how long I have to live with this system—I will never accept it," he said. Martin would grow up feeling the same way as his father.

WHITE ONLY

Martin was a very good student. He even skipped two grades. Before starting Morehouse College at the age of fifteen, he took a summer job in Connecticut. Things were different there for black people. In the North, black and white children went to the same schools. There were no separate water fountains. Everyone could shop in the same stores.

Martin Luther King Jr. had a dream. He dreamed that these things could happen in the South, too. Was there a way he could help people change the laws to make this dream come true?

Martin decided to spend his life helping black people. He thought perhaps if he became a minister, he could reach people with his words, so he became an assistant minister at his father's church and went to seminary.

Later, Martin entered Boston University. There he met Coretta Scott, who was studying to be a singer. On their first date, they talked about how hard it was to be black in the United States. They talked about how people could live together in peace instead. After only one hour, Martin was sure he would marry Coretta one day. And he did!

After Martin and Coretta got married, a letter arrived from a church in Montgomery, Alabama. The church leaders invited Martin to give a sermon there. If he did a good job, they would make him their minister.

On a clear winter day, Martin drove from Boston to Montgomery. He knew his words had to come from his heart. He knew he could help people find strength to live out their faith. And Martin got the job.

With his words, Martin told church members to go out and vote. Voting was one way to change unfair laws against black people.

With his words, Martin helped organize protests. He told black people not to ride the buses in Alabama. Martin and others didn't think it was fair for black people to be forced to ride in the back.

And with his silence, Martin and many others sat at "whites only" lunch counters.

One summer day, thousands of people
traveled to Washington, D.C., for the March
on Washington for Jobs and Freedom.
Martin was the last to speak that day.

"I have a dream," his voice boomed, "that my four little children will one day live in a nation where they will not be judged by the color of their skin, but by the content of their character."

Thousands of other people shared Martin's dream. Hand in hand, they walked through quiet valleys, over steep hills, and along busy highways, their hearts filled with hope for equality.

Martin won important awards for his work. Sadly, he did not live to see all his dreams come true. But he did see the day when the laws were changed so that Americans of all colors were allowed to go to school together, sit together in restaurants, and shop at the same stores.

Each day, people honor him when they visit
his memorial statue in Washington, D.C.

Martin Luther King Jr. will
be forever remembered as a
leader who fought for equal
rights and freedom for all. In
many places around the world,
this fight continues—and
Martin's words and dreams
live on.